Burn the Ships

Leading in a World Without Compassion

Andrew S. Keen

Written and Published in the United States of America

All questions or requests should be directed to:
PO Box 691 New Albany, OH 43054 or
leadingwithcompassion@gmail.com

Cover Design by Betsabé Garcia
Author Photograph by Ploof Photography

Paperback ISBN: 978-1-7356286-0-8
ebook ISBN: 978-1-7356286-1-5

Library of Congress Control Number: 2020916540

For all those who believed in my potential,
invested in my future, and taught me what it
means to lead

CONTENTS

FOREWARD

One of the first things you'll notice in any bookstore is an overwhelming number of books offering to teach you the secrets of leadership. The subject of leadership is one that has eluded mastery throughout the history of the profession. (You'll notice I'll largely choose not to use the word management throughout this book, and for good reason.)

If we step back for a minute and think about management, it's a profession we created: a result of Industrial Age scale and mass production. It's not a natural state that exists in our relationships with others. Leadership, on the other hand, is.[1] It's something we seek out in our lives; and when we find leaders we want to follow, we do so without fear (though not without disagreement at times). Leadership ties us together at a deeper level and is not something we can dictate for others. You can be told who your manager is; you have to decide if that manager is your leader. To put it another way, management is assigned; to follow is a choice.

Management is a subset of leadership. It's required for organizational success and to reach your objectives. However, it defines itself by a focus on outcomes. All that matters is to achieve what we were assigned at an acceptable cost. What it struggles to recognize at times is the value of people within an organization.

Therefore, leadership is perhaps the most critical element to an organization's success, regardless of the industry or profit objectives. Perhaps cliché, but also true: people don't leave organizations, they leave leaders. With this in mind, in a world where

---

[1] Slim, Sir William "Leadership in Management." *Australian Army Journal*, no. 102, 1957, pp. 5-13 researchcentre.army.gov.au/sites/default/files/ aaj_102_nov_1957_0.pdf. Accessed 18 Aug. 2020.

knowledge and human capital are the most important inputs to success, how we lead our teams has increasingly become the key.

Accordingly, numerous people have attempted to distill leadership into a few key principles that if you adopt them, will make you a great leader. As with most things in life, nothing's that easy. Leadership is not innate, it's not something we're born with, but it is something we can aspire to. It requires study, practice, and continued investment, just as though you were learning to play an instrument. It's also something we will never truly master. Why? The world changes every day and people change with it. Accordingly, your approach to leadership must change as well. Will some people be further ahead based on the lessons learned early in life? Absolutely. But at its core, leadership in today's world is more about offering something we've lost: humility and respect.

I've often thought that I'm not qualified to offer guidance to others on how to lead successfully. I believe I've been successful in building strong teams ready to step up when required. But what makes me someone who can pass on advice to others? I'm not a C-level executive, governmental official, professor, doctor, consultant or other person we typically look to for guidance on weighty matters. No, I'm simply a man who has developed a perspective on leadership over the last two decades. I've been formally educated in management, attended corporate development programs, and read many of those books I referenced at the start. However, in the end I have found my own approach to leadership that seems out of step with most of what I've seen in my small part of the world today.

That is the point of this endeavor: to put into print that which has served me and my teams well to this point in my career. My sincere hope is to pass on what I've learned through trial, error, and feedback from those I've been honored to lead, so that those who pick this book up in the future might start further along the path than I.

1

"BURN THE SHIPS" AND OUR WORLD

The phrase "Burn the Ships" has a storied history largely associated with a dedication to the mission so great that people are willing to eliminate all means of retreat. In 334 B.C., Alexander the Great landed on the shores of modern day Turkey intent on conquering Darius III and ending the Persian Empire. Over time the story has evolved to reflect a decision by Alexander to burn his ships in order to demonstrate his commitment to the cause, telling his armies they would return home on

Persian ships. While history always remembers a great story, published accounts reflect a much more rational approach to military tactics. As he was exclusively conducting a land campaign, the fleet was largely useless and expensive to maintain. At an estimated cost of sixty to ninety thousand dollars per month,[2] before food and supplies, Alexander's conquests had not yielded the funds required to support such an expense. Pragmatic as ever, Alexander disbanded his fleet and sent his ships back to their home ports.[3]

While the solution may not have the same flourish as enjoying a bonfire for the ages, the result was the same. Alexander now had his army stranded on the Asian side of the Hellespont with only the supplies they brought and whatever they could scavenge as they marched. He now faced conquering the Persian Empire with no hope of rescue or retreat. This may seem mad as opposed to courageous, but as we all know, history is written by the victor. Of course, Alexander the Great went on

---

[2] Adjusting for inflation since its original publication this would equate to $1.5 - $2.6 million per month.

[3] Wheeler, Benjamin Ide. *Alexander the Great; the Merging of East and West in Universal History.* United States, G.P. Putnam's Sons, 1904.

to defeat the Persians and occupy Babylon before continuing his campaign east.

Another example from history comes from 1519 when Hernán Cortés landed near Veracruz in modern day Mexico. The story goes that, upon arrival, focused on conquering the Aztec capital of Tenochtitlan, Cortés ordered the firing of his ships[4] to force his men deep into enemy territory. Once again, with no chance of escape or retreat, his army had no choice but to complete its mission or perish in the jungles of Mesoamerica. Unfortunately, the sinking of his fleet was not driven by a laser-like focus on his objective, but a much more immediate concern: to prevent men loyal to the Governor of Cuba from mutinying, taking possession of a ship, and returning to the Spanish-held island. Though it doesn't have the same romantic quality, Cortés did indeed sink his ships, claiming they were no longer able to sail safely.[5]

---

[4] While it has become part of the popular retelling, many historians believe that Cortés didn't actually burn his ships, but sank them via other means.

[5] Díaz del Castillo, Bernal, et al. *The True History of the Conquest of New Spain*. United Kingdom, Hakluyt society, 1908.

Burn the Ships

So two of our most vivid historical examples of courageous, committed, and focused leaders burning their ships in a dramatic tour de force aren't quite true. This doesn't matter, though, as the results and the impact to their armies were the same. You have a group of men, far from the safety of home, now stranded in a foreign land with no option but to move ahead. There is no retreat, no chance to pause and resupply; and those who are not strong enough to continue are left to the mercies of the wilds beyond.

Can you imagine how the Macedonians must have felt as they stood on the beach watching their only means of escape disappear beyond the horizon? When Cortés handed the torches out and gave the order to fire the ships, how many might have thought about throwing them in the ocean instead of the hold? Were they anxious or even terrified of what might lie ahead? Of course, none would ever admit that to the others. As supplies start to run low or the first defeats set in, confidence in leadership quickly follows. They had a forced dependency on their leader which likely left many of them thinking, "This isn't what I signed up for." While at times Alexander the Great and Cortés are glorified for the commitment their acts forced among their armies, how might history remember them had their armies fallen, and, faced with no means of retreat, been left to slaughter?

The relevance to today's world couldn't be more apt. We now live and work in a world where the ships have been burned and we have no option to retreat. The continued acceleration of technology has brought us into an age where we are "on" 24/7 with no chance to pause, step back to recover, resupply, and prepare for the next engagement. Any mistakes we make are known immediately; and not just in our communities, but around the globe. At the same time, as a people we've lost all tolerance for error and have no pity for those we push to the side in our pursuits. People now become dedicated to a position, hardened and reinforced by likeminded individuals. This has left us with a new normal: single-minded focus on an outcome, with a willingness to sacrifice all to see it achieved. This leaves us operating in a world of extremes, where compassion is lacking and compromise a lost art. Sound familiar?

This is the backdrop through which we are challenged to lead. The safety nets have been pulled and we have to personally survive each day while at the same time marshaling others to achieve greater things.

2

THE IMPACT ON OUR PEOPLE AND CULTURE

It's a pretty bleak picture, but also the reality of how we live. The promise of a connected world has been realized in many ways, but it has come at the cost of our humanity. We have embraced the benefits of technology as an economic and productivity lever, but failed to adjust the lens through which we lead to account for the human impact. No matter how much we augment people with tools and information to increase their capabilities, in the end they are still a person with hopes, dreams, fears, and, yes, limitations. The human impact in a "Burn the Ships" world is material and requires us to understand how people perceive it if we are to lead them in it.

The increased demands on each of us is the easiest place to start. Technology has had a profound impact on our world throughout history and has revolutionized all aspects of our lives. The pace of change has accelerated in the last century to where things once considered fiction become reality in one lifetime. Many of us have lived half a lifetime and seen the world progress from typewriters, to mainframes, on to personal computing, then mobile, and now the internet of things. The only question is not what can be added to the network, but how much it will cost to bring to market. In the span of one generation's working life, this accounts for a dizzying amount of change in how people perform their jobs. This doesn't even begin to account for the impact in how these changes affect them personally and how it redefines our unwritten contract between team and leader.

The Impact on Our People and Culture

The application of processing power and connectivity to the workplace has increased the demands on each of us across our professional and personal lives. These elements are no longer separate from each other as we have blurred the lines between what it means to be "at work" or "at home." We no longer leave work behind for the day and begin the physical separation from our obligations. Our mobile devices ensure we're available 24/7 to our colleagues and employers and there is no excuse for not dealing with the next emergency no matter the time or place. Not to mention the fact that the definition of emergency, and thus need for immediate action, continues to expand.

The expectation of working in our world today is not that a company has purchased 40 hours of our lives each week, but also that they have an option on the remaining waking hours. This has understandably increased the strain on our people, their families, and ourselves, directly translating into fatigue and burnout. It even changes how we interact with one another. Focusing on the rapid resolution of our immediate needs, we disregard the value of connecting with others, compromising our ability to empathize, and contributing to our loss of compassion.

The amount of information we must consume and react to on a daily basis continues to increase every year as well. This is indicative of the 24/7 world we live in, but it also impacts our ability and willingness to research and truly understand an issue. We seek out the quick summary, the bullet points, or the "for dummies" version of a topic to quickly get up to speed and move on to the next set of data we have to understand. While it generally means we are the most educated and informed generation in our shared history, we have to ask, "To what benefit?" If we only take the time to understand a topic superficially, because we can't afford any more, how can we really understand the nuances and implications of it? This leads us to a difficult realization. We are making decisions with far reaching implications based on a flawed belief that we are qualified to do so. This translates directly to more mistakes being made in a world where we aren't willing to take the time to understand why they happened at all. We don't believe we have the time to look to yesterday when tomorrow is already here. If we're not willing to understand why the mistake happened, then the only alternative is to blame the person who made it. Thus, we increasingly fear errors and try to hide our failures from all involved. It is yet another ramification of compassion lost.

The pace of change in the world extends far beyond technology. The impact to our fields of expertise and what is required to remain relevant in workplaces creates additional pressure on our people. Rather than face perhaps one or two requirements to up-skill during their career, failure to continue to invest in yourself each and every year will result in quickly becoming obsolete. It doesn't matter at what level you sit within an organization, there is no concept of having "made it" to where you no longer have to worry. This translates to an inherent fear in our workplaces that impacts our team dynamics and partnership. This fear is reinforced by the routine layoffs we have begun to see in our firms as standard year over year reductions are built into financial plans based on expected, and required, efficiency gains. If our team members are constantly worried about their jobs, then they naturally will begin to operate for personal gain as opposed to the collective good. At our core, we are self-interested and will take actions to protect ourselves before helping others.

The continued reduction in workforce also translates to reduced opportunities for advancement. Career paths are reduced as organizational hierarchies flatten. When openings do occur they are not filled but eliminated, and people begin to lose faith in a future with the firm. Retention of our highest talent individuals becomes increasingly challenging as they begin to believe the only chance to achieve their goals is to seek opportunities elsewhere. Workforce reduction also translates to increased competition for the few promotions that remain in what becomes a zero sum game. This further damages our culture and our teams as we begin to realize that someone else must lose so I can win.

If these changes were not enough, we also cannot ignore the implications of what is happening in our broader world, the one that exists outside the four walls of our office and our sphere of control. Politics, religion, cultural differences, the list goes on, but we have to acknowledge that our world continues to become more polarized. Somewhere along the way we have lost the ability to respectfully disagree with one another and co-exist in harmony, finding a middle ground. Now we assume negative or at best neutral intent from those we interact with and have established a mindset of "us vs them" when we disagree. While we may try to treat our workplaces as a neutral ground, independent of the world around us, we cannot ignore the outside world. Ignoring this leads us to a "hands off" approach at best to certain subjects or at worst treating them as taboo. While it may be hidden beneath the surface of political correctness, this polarization is present within our workplaces waiting for the opportunity to impact our people, our productivity, and our hard fought for culture.

The changing world has resulted in "Burn the Ships" leaders taking over our teams. These types of leaders have allowed the world around them to dictate how they will lead. In many ways, while they likely didn't make a conscious decision to lead in this manner, they went with the flow. As the world changed, they didn't want to fight it; because, like all of us, the demands on them increased as well. Perhaps they simply didn't have the time or energy to invest in creating a counter culture. Or perhaps they were engaged in their own battles for survival and relevance as they had to up-skill themselves to operate in today's world. Regardless, they have reacted to the increased competition and demands for more efficient operations by treating their teams as inherently replaceable, as they were faced with constant "rack and stack" performance management cycles and shrinking budgets. These leaders have reduced their commitment to creating a real team —the kind we know from our personal lives—one deeply invested in and dependent on each other; dedicated to their collective success.

The "Burn the Ships" leader can be summarized as the natural outcome of a world without compassion. Eliminating this core component of the human experience from our professional lives results in the following type of leader:

- Focused on their own success and using the team as a tool to achieve it
- Sees internal competition as beneficial, not destructive to achieving objectives
- Believes talent is replaceable and, accordingly, teams are temporary
- Assumes personal lives are not relevant to our professional ones
- Achieves the objective at all costs, no matter what it means
- Protects themselves when things go wrong

The Impact on Our People and Culture

This type of leader will be successful for a time, but they will sacrifice their people along the way, either through attrition of high-quality talent, or by blaming them when things go wrong. Like our earlier examples, they are leading a forced march forward with no option to rest or retreat. People will only follow this leader until success begins to fade, they can no longer keep up with the pace that has been set, or they are cast aside to further the leader's goals.

The world we live in has changed dramatically to the benefit of many, but to the detriment of our workplaces. What we need today is a new class of leaders: people who refuse to accept that we cannot fight the currents battering us. Who believe we can lead differently in an environment that would have us abandon our people to the harsh realities of this world. Who understand that compassion has a place in our lives; and who realize that our lives don't begin and end as soon as we walk through the office door.

3

THE IMPACT ON HOW WE LEAD

In a world where compassion has lost its value in business, the way to challenge our unacceptable status quo is to reject it. To decide to lead with our teams' best interests at heart and with a view to the future. Being a compassionate leader is actually the only way to achieve long lasting success in our world. Who would you rather work for: a hard driving leader who treats their team as replaceable resources, or someone who actually cares about your well being and wants to help you achieve your goals? We all know the answer. It's about changing your view to one that focuses on the collective good rather than a traditional view focused solely on outcome at all cost.

The "Burn the Ships" approach to delivery defines itself by a focus on outcomes. It assumes that people are just one factor of production when, in fact, that idea belongs to a time in our history that is long gone. In the past, we could train an individual to do a job quickly and cheaply. People remained in one location, and their careers were largely spent with one company, and perhaps even performing only one job. This combination allowed leaders to take their teams for granted knowing they could replace them and that their options to leave were limited.

The skills required for success in today's economy are far more unique and knowledge based. Because of this, team members cannot be easily substituted. Additionally, talent mobility is no longer a constraint, but an asset. The best talent can and will move to find the right opportunity, with the right support structure for success. If you can provide that structure, you will find talent knocking at the door to join your team. Today, our people are our greatest asset and source of competitive advantage. Accordingly, your goal should not just be to lead, but to create followers. Followership is the sole choice of the individual and, accordingly, the ultimate measure of success. If someone chooses to follow, it's the highest form of praise for and validation of your leadership. This translates to a greater commitment to your objectives, a presumption of positive intentions, and a willingness to sacrifice in order to support you, not to mention a strong desire to continue to work for you. It's worth noting that no formal leadership role is required to embrace this approach. You truly can lead from any seat if people are willing to follow.

The move from ship burning to compassion is not an easy journey to undertake, but it's one that can create a sustainable competitive advantage if you fully embrace it. You can create an environment where compassion is a freely available and respected. This by itself will set you apart from many leaders in today's world, sadly, but it's far from the only benefit. Compassion is foundational to creating a meaningful environmental change for your team. If we eliminate fear and create a place where people can experiment, fail, and learn, we have the start of a successful team dynamic. This will allow your teams to challenge existing norms, explore new ways of doing things, grow personally and professionally, and ultimately succeed. It's a refreshing change from the world they know and lived (or perhaps survived is a better description) in previously. If you commit to creating this environment, the best people will gravitate toward you, your team will have no shortage of candidates for open positions, and you will of course benefit as a result.

This creates a different problem though. You have to become that leader you'd want to work for. This requires a commitment probably far beyond one you've been willing to make to your team so far. Truly leading, instead of managing by another name, requires a fundamental shift in your mindset. It requires you to put your own ego and feeling of entitlement aside and look at your job differently. You are not empowered but entrusted with a group of people who will look to you for guidance, support, and protection from the world around them. Your team is not there to work for you: you are there to work for your team. Stop and take a minute to think about what that means. By embracing this view of your job, you create an environment where people see that for all they give, they reap benefits as well. They have a stronger connection to their team and the firm, they see continued investment in themselves, and they know they are better for the experience. This is much harder to achieve, though, as it requires a person who understands that whosoever wishes to lead must first serve.

It's become a bit of a cliché in today's world, but a servant mindset is a critical component to a commitment to lead with compassion. This is a lesson in extremes though as successful application requires balancing opposing positions on a regular basis. It is natural to think of self-preservation and how to maximize benefit for yourself first. The power of compassionate leadership is to set aside the inherent drive to achieve your goals and see personal benefit as an outcome, not a primary objective to achieve.

4

KEY TENETS OF COMPASSIONATE LEADERSHIP

You've come this far. What matters is that this means you care. You've realized something is missing in how you lead your teams and likely in how you are led as well. That something is *compassion*. It starts with a concept that's at the core of how we operate at the office: the concept of business vs personal. The notion that we have two lives that are completely separate, and as soon as we walk in the front door or login remotely, we switch from our personal persona to business. This is a really hard reality to grapple with because likely it's how you were taught to lead. "It's not personal, it's just business," I'm sure you've all heard or said yourself at some point in your career.

"It's just business" is no more

This is the first concept we have to kill if we're going to be a compassionate leader. We have to accept that business is personal. It's based on people, and as a result it comes with all the same challenges, complications, and baggage we deal with throughout our lives. This notion that "it's just business" is an excuse we use to protect ourselves; to allow us as leaders to separate ourselves from our decisions and the very real outcomes they have on our teams. There is a legitimate need to build in some level of separation as we can't empathize fully or we'd never make a difficult decision for the good of the whole. However, as leaders, we also have to eliminate the easy excuses from our tool kits.

This is a hard transition to make as you start on your journey. You have to be willing to first, accept ownership for how your decisions impact the whole person (professional and personal) and second, give more of yourself, your personal side, to your team. This second part can be very difficult, even more so for introverts, as it comes at an emotional toll for the leader. Now you have to allow yourself to feel, and to let others see it too, where before being a stoic "nothing else matters" professional was all that was required. Allowing others to see how you're feeling is not a sign of weakness. To the contrary, it validates your message about being willing to bring your whole self to work, and humanizes you to your team. Relationships take effort, trust, and a genuine connection. You can't connect with your team in a meaningful way unless you let them see the real you too.

One way to quickly establish this framework with your team is to engage in an "ask me anything" session. Set up an hour with them, preferably in person or by video to further personalize the discussion, with no agenda. Positioning the discussion as one with no topic off limits will put a lot of teams ill at ease. Unused to interacting with their leadership in this way, they expect you to enforce a level of separation, which you are eliminating with this approach. One way to help start the discussion is to allow people to submit some anonymous questions as conversation starters, but be prepared to proactively start sharing your personal and professional history to get things started. Make sure to offer some thoughts on your family, upbringing, social activities, or other items that have nothing to do with your professional relationship. This will set the stage with your team that you are bringing your whole self to work, and they can too.

Earn the Right to Lead

We've all seen it happen: someone gets promoted to a position of leadership, having left a trail of destruction behind them. They may have gotten across the goal line, but at the cost of damaged relationships and unsustainable methods. It leaves everyone else wondering, "Why do we reward that behavior?" It's corrosive to the culture, and if we're not careful, it leads to others believing that this is the right way to act. We can get a lot done in the short term if we don't care who we hurt in the process. This is far from a sustainable approach to success though. As Boris Yeltsin put it, you can build a throne with bayonets, but you can't sit on it for long.[6]

This is why compassionate leadership starts before you ever get the opportunity to lead a team or organization. You have to start your journey by understanding that you have to earn the right to lead others. Sure, you could get there by taking credit for others' work, bullying people to accomplish your objectives on budget and ahead of schedule, or by simply not caring about who you hurt in the process. This is not earning the right to lead though, especially if you work in a firm that historically promotes from within. As we stated at the beginning of this chapter, this is not just business, this is about people; and people have a long memory. They will remember how you treated them in the past. They will choose to honor your accomplishments, or they will choose to disparage them to others. Also, people will prejudge your qualifications to lead others based on how you led when you had no formal authority. The reputation

---

[6] Staff and Agencies. "The wit and wisdom of Boris." *The Guardian,* Independent Digital News and Media, 23 Apr. 2007, www.theguardian.com/world/2007/apr/23/russia2. Accessed 24 Aug. 2020. (Courtesy of Guardian News & Media Ltd - Open License)

you build for yourself will be key to your ability to lead once the opportunity comes. The history of how you got the opportunity to lead is just as important as what you do and how you act when you get there.

Some of you may be the reluctant boss, selected for the role because of your technical or subject matter expertise. Many corporations have a misplaced belief that if you were the best performer within your team, you must be the best person to lead them. There is some truth to this when knowledge of the process is critical to success. However, this creates a challenging set of circumstances for compassionate leaders to develop unless they work hard to pivot from the expert to the leader. Leadership and functional knowledge skills are not interchangeable, but the good news is leading people starts with people recognizing why you were selected to lead, and you likely have a head start since you were seen as the best at what you do.

Earlier, we touched on the fact that the goal and ultimate measure of success is followership. While you may be granted formal authority over your team, mere authority will not generate commitment or allow you to realize the full potential of your workforce. In fact, without spending the time to build followers you will get the minimum possible from your teams. While you may still have some stars who are working toward their next role, the vast majority of your staff will not give you their all. Over 50% of your team is likely made up of tenured people who are happy in their jobs and are not looking to do more. They are critical to your success, for without them nothing gets done, but they aren't going to be self-motivated to outperform. What incentive do they have to give more than what is required to get their yearly bonus or to avoid getting fired? This is why you have to start with generating the buy-in and agreement that you are qualified to lead them. Unfortunately, it's not as simple as saying, "Hey, I'm in charge now." So how do we earn the right to lead? We start with our mindset about leadership in general and the emotional bond or lack thereof this creates.

You are not empowered, you are entrusted

There is a historical view in corporate history of the do-nothing boss who looks great in meetings, but never seems to actually get any work done. Whether it's a movie like *Office Space* or any one of hundreds of *Dilbert* cartoons, we all know the type of boss we're talking about. This is why as a compassionate leader you need to realize that you are not empowered, but entrusted. The distinction is an important one, as many people step into a role of authority with a view of empowerment. "I have power over a group of people, and they are here to do what I need to meet our goals." This couldn't be farther from the truth. As a compassionate leader, you are entrusted with a group of people to achieve an organizational objective. You have been given responsibility for the labor and resulting quality of life that constitutes most of a person's waking hours. In addition, you have responsibility for supporting their dreams, both personal and professional; protecting them when appropriate; and at the same time holding them accountable for their work. I'm sure you'd agree, when viewed through this lens, this is a large burden to bear.

When you adopt a mindset of being entrusted with a group of people, your entire approach to leading them will change. You will set your priorities differently and you will begin to spend more time investing in helping them achieve their goals rather than driving them to achieve yours. Leaders also simply treat people differently when they see themselves in a servant role. Think about how you might treat a friend or a loved one in their time of need. Why do we treat them with so much more care than those in our professional circles? We likely spend less time with them than our teams or coworkers, so it can't be because of a time investment. It's because we have allowed ourselves to grow close to them, to empathize with their needs, and to feel a sense of duty to them.

While clearly we cannot have the same relationships in the office, as we have to maintain some distance from our teams, this is the gulf we're trying to close when we talk about being entrusted. As leaders, we are there to support and care about their well being. In doing so, we create a shared commitment to each other; and as a result, we get the benefit of their best work. People want to give all they have for those who they know have their best interests at heart. This is human nature at its finest. They also are loyal to leaders like this, following them when they take on new roles. Adopting the view that you are not empowered but entrusted also creates a legacy. Your team will become your greatest advocates. The best support for your own career is a team who sells your virtues. Shifting your mindset is just one part of earning the right to lead. The next requires you to live it.

Get in the dirt

Too often as leaders rise through the ranks they start to believe certain jobs are beneath them. This is indicative of an empowered mindset as opposed to one of service. It is perhaps one of the quickest ways to sacrifice some of the gains you've made in building a culture of followership, as people will see how you take advantage of your position when it matters to you. How often are you willing to do the grunt work? Think about the last time you had to work a release weekend, or deal with an issue in the middle of the night. Was your leader there for you? Did they dial into the calls or come into the office to check in? How would it have made you feel if they did? Would you have felt like you were all in this together? Would you have believed there was a greater commitment to you, your work, and a shared belief in its importance?

It doesn't have to be a regular occurrence, but even just once a quarter has a meaningful impact on how your team views you as a leader. They see that you're willing to get in the dirt and get the job done, no matter what it takes. They'll also tell others, further reinforcing your reputation and the commitment of your team. In fact, many times you'll find that a member of your team volunteers to do the work in your stead because they know you have "better things to do" and they respect the fact you're willing to get back in the trenches with them. Put simply, never ask your team to do anything you wouldn't do yourself.

You will be wrong…just admit it

Some of you may have it in your minds that as a leader we have to aways be right. We can't afford to lose credibility by admitting we were wrong, and look for any excuse to avoid doing so. In fact, this is the worst thing we can do as leaders. We do not know it all, nor are we perfect. We can just hope to get it right more than we get it wrong. Admitting when you're wrong will engender more respect among your team as you acknowledge your own shortcomings. It serves to humanize you, it allows you to show that you value being proven wrong, and it builds a culture of openness where admitting fault is okay. This is even more important when errors happen deeper in your organization and rapid escalation is critical to mitigate the potential far-reaching implications. By admitting when you are wrong, you make it okay for others to do the same. Of course, owning up to mistakes does not mean there will not be consequences, depending on the severity, but if you haven't created a culture that supports owning up to them, they are guaranteed to be far worse than if they had been addressed earlier.

Another version of admitting when you're wrong can take the form of a challenge to your team. As leaders, we all have to make decisions about any number of different questions in a given day. One of the most powerful statements when there is disagreement about the path ahead is "I would love to be proven wrong." You have to really mean it, and pick and choose when it is appropriate to use, but this can be an effective tool to challenge your team to prove you wrong. This will motivate them to do just that and show you why your belief was mistaken. Honoring them when they do so can be a powerful engagement and motivation tool for the entire organization as it further demonstrates your openness to being proven human.

This may be hard for some of you to do. This is when we are the most vulnerable personally, which is also why it is a powerful action toward leading with compassion. When you allow yourself to be vulnerable with others, they in turn will be more willing to offer the same to you. Owning your mistakes further establishes your right to lead and at the same time contributes to a critical element of the culture you need in order to protect yourself and your organization.

Protect and respect your team

This section may seem repetitive at this point, but it's critical to remember that you are here to serve your team. Part of that is to protect them from the numerous forces that would harm them each day. This could come in the form of unreasonable performance demands, pressure to terminate employees when mistakes happen, restructuring discussions, etc. The list of possible harms could consume another twenty pages. However, your job is the same: to protect them so they can do their best work. Fear is catastrophic to productivity; and if your team is focused on what could happen, they aren't focused on what needs to be done. This results in a self-reinforcing downward spiral impacting performance, and accordingly, the perception of their continued value to the enterprise. In some cases, the fear of what could happen becomes a self-fulfilling prophesy.

Another component of protecting your team is having a vision for the future. One of the challenging elements of establishing a vision is attempting to predict how the world will change in the years ahead. Which new technologies will impact how we interact with customers or how we work each day? You will likely be wrong, but what is important is that you have a vision you are willing to articulate and prepare your team for. One thing we can know with certainty is that the world will be different than it is today, and if you don't have a vision you are guaranteed to be wrong.

Protecting your team also requires the courage to challenge your own leaders. Managerial courage can take many forms, but at its core it is about being willing to put your position or reputation on the line to do the right thing. To be willing to stand up to your senior leadership when the demands become too great or when decisions are at odds with the culture of the organization. This is a balancing act as you have to know when to push back and when to allow the extra pressure to be applied for the good of the organization as a whole.

People by nature crave stability, and in fact, need it to perform at their best. Psychologist Abraham Maslow identified "safety" as one of our base needs.[7] When it is not met, motivation and performance decrease. While the original theory referred to physical safety, it's just as applicable to our ability to perform at work. For example, when we see senior leadership change, for better or worse, it forces us to reevaluate our place in the organization and how our contributions are perceived. Has my place and influence or power changed? Am I now at greater risk as the relationship investments I have made over time are zeroed out, making me more vulnerable? While we may not consciously think about these types of questions when the unexpected happens, at its core, the feeling your team is reacting to is the loss of safety. Change is inevitable: we can't prevent it, but we can control our response. To paraphrase Julius Caesar, no one is so brave that they are not shaken

---

[7] Maslow, A. H. (1943). A theory of human motivation. *Psychological Review, 50*(4), 370–396. https://doi.org/10.1037/h0054346. Accessed 2 Sept. 2020. (Public Domain)

by the unexpected.[8] It's up to the compassionate leader to help their team navigate the rapidly changing nature of our workplaces and protect them, at times even from themselves. While we'll address some of the more challenging elements that impact your team later, the compassionate leader sees their primary job as the protection of their team.

They may be accountable, but you are responsible

The funny thing about leading with compassion is that no matter how large your organization, how many layers of leaders may be beneath you with their own teams, you are still responsible for everything that happens. You have delegated accountability for the activities, but not the responsibility for the result. You may wonder why. Didn't we hire people so they would be responsible for the work and I could focus on something else? The short answer is no. When you made the hire decision or allowed them to remain on your team, you made a decision to trust that individual with a

---

[8]Caesar, Julius. *Commentaries on the Gallic and Civil Wars: With the Supplementary Books Attributed to Hirtius, Including the Alexandrian, African, and Spanish Wars.* United States, Harper Brothers, 1885.

portion of your authority. It was your decision to entrust them with the delivery of a task or leadership of a team. Accordingly, you are responsible for their failures just as you get credit for their successes. As a compassionate leader, you cannot shirk your ownership of everything that occurs within your organization, regardless of whether you were directly engaged in the activity.

It can be tempting to assign blame to the individual who made an error, but you have to remember that part of your job is to provide a space for growth, and failure is a part of that process. If you think back on your own career there are likely plenty of examples of times you failed while trying to learn something new or better understand the nuances of a process. Did your leader at the time blame you, telling everyone else you were at fault, and now they had to fix it? Or did they coach you regarding what went wrong, while shouldering the blame with you, and enlisting your help in making things right? Even if your experience was the former, wouldn't you have wished to work for someone who understood they were responsible even if you were accountable for the error? Being responsible for everything that happens within your organization is part of the burden of leadership, but it is also one of the benefits. When you take responsibility for the teams failures, your team will want to share their successes with you too. The mindset of "rising and falling" together further reinforces a culture of mutual support, safety, and trust.

Honest and Ethical - None of this matters without it

Finally, you can forget everything you've read so far about earning the right to lead if you don't ensure you are honest and ethical in all your dealings. Nothing hurts people more or destroys trust faster than a leader who doesn't operate in a forthright manner. Additionally, no one wants to follow a leader whom they cannot trust or who doesn't live what they preach. There will always be times when you have information you cannot share which may impact your team. They know this and understand, though they may not like it. You should always share what information you can, while protecting the trust placed in you by others, and acknowledging when there are some things you just can't discuss. Sharing more will help maintain trust in all times, not just difficult ones. The greater risk is the perception that you are hiding things from your team.

In times of severe organizational stress or when they fear for their jobs your investments in compassionate leadership will really bear fruit. Your team will place their trust in you and continue to perform as they know you have their best interests at heart and will tell them what you can when you can. The impact on team dynamics cannot be overstated. While other teams will be floundering, yours will continue like nothing is going on, further establishing your reputation for leadership.

———————

While these practices will help you earn the right to lead with your teams, you must genuinely believe in them. They cannot be faked: your team will see through you quickly. You must live them every day. That is not to say that we all don't make mistakes and slip back into a "Burn the Ships" mentality, but we have to quickly identify when it happens, own it, and take action to rectify it going forward. If you've earned the right to lead with your team you will have also have built a reserve of goodwill. This is not an inexhaustible source though and it will only suffer so many mistakes before your team begins to believe you aren't committed to leading with compassion. The transition to compassionate leadership is a journey that requires significant amounts of self-reflection and, at times, fighting the urge to protect yourself before others. Allow yourself the opportunity to learn and grow as a leader when you do make mistakes. Leading with compassion means offering it to yourself as well.

5

BUILDING A TEAM THAT WON'T RETREAT

It doesn't matter what type of leader you have been to this point: building a successful team is critical to your continued success. Leading with compassion doesn't mean you can't build a team that won't retreat. You don't have to "Burn the Ships" to get them on board with your goals and achieve victories that have yet to be won. What you must do is invest the time and effort to find people who willingly step in line beside you no matter the challenge ahead. It all starts with selecting the right people. After that, it's how you continue to earn the right to lead with them over time.

The hardest decisions we make as leaders are not strategic objectives or executional approaches. It's who we hire and empower to do the job. These decisions have far-reaching consequences and getting just one wrong can severely impact your team, culture, and you. If you don't find the hire decision the most difficult one in your day, think about why. As you embrace the principles of compassionate leadership, your team will become a core part of your day-to-day life. These are the people you are going to invest in and entrust with your reputation and authority, and who will ultimately determine your future with the firm. You must ensure that you put the right people in the right roles and trust them to execute on your behalf.

Take a moment to consider hiring someone to care for your loved ones. How much time would you spend vetting each candidate? Would you want to know their complete history to identify any potential red flags? What about knowing how they would fit in with those they would be caring for? How many times would you question your decision or be afraid you'd never forgive yourself if something happened based on your selection? Choosing a new team member is no different. Shouldn't the most important decision you make at the office be who you choose to be part of your team?

Many firms use a slate model to hire people for teams, asking numerous stakeholders or other leaders to interview in addition to the hiring manager. While not inherently wrong, this approach does not support compassionate leadership for two reasons. First, it reduces your authority to hire the best qualified candidate for your team as others can override your decision. Second, it removes your sense of ownership and accountability for making sure the right decision is made. It's natural to seek ways to cover ourselves or even to find others to blame if a decision doesn't play out as we had hoped. A slate approach provides the mechanism to do so by being able to point to others who agreed along the way. Freedom from the consequences of the hiring decision can lead you to make compromises you otherwise would refuse if there was no one to blame but yourself. Even if your firm still requires a slate based process, you can apply these principles. Have the courage to take full ownership of the decision, be willing to advocate for your choice against any opposition, and accept the consequences of your decision accordingly. While there are other negative outcomes — for example, lengthening the hiring process, potentially allowing others to make offers to your candidates — these two are the most critical implications for you and your team.

This doesn't mean that at times getting additional senior level input isn't recommended or appropriate: for example, when the role will require the individual to matrix or dotted line report to an additional leader in the organization, or when a high degree of technical knowledge is required for success and you do not possess the required skill set to evaluate their competence. However, it must be in support of the candidate's success in the role, not to alleviate your fear of making the wrong call.

One exception to this rule is having members of your team perform a peer interview as part of the process. How new team members match the culture and fit in with the larger team will be an important element to their success and retention.

Building a Team That Won't Retreat

Culture mismatch is often one of the biggest reasons people are unsuccessful in transitioning into new roles, and these types of sessions can help better evaluate fit than a leader-candidate discussion. Culture is viewed very differently based on where you sit in the organization, and it's best communicated and evaluated at a peer to peer level. This doesn't mean that you cannot override your team's opinion. Again, this is your decision, but getting an additional point of view from your team cannot hurt, as long as it doesn't overly extend the selection process.

While getting qualified candidates to apply can be a challenge in itself, if you have earned the right to lead with your current team you likely will have no trouble finding interested candidates. Your team will become your best recruiters as over time they build your brand for you. Everyone at a firm knows who they want to work for and who they don't. Of course, this doesn't mean your applicants will be qualified. Selecting the right person still falls solely on you and will require you to dedicate a significant portion of time to the process.

Your success in finding the right people for a driven team starts with writing the job requisition.

How much time did you spend putting it together? Did you just take a generic Human Resources outline for a given role, add a few sentences, and post it? If you don't spend the time to holistically articulate who you are looking for, the skills they need, and the type of challenges they will need to tackle, then you will not get the right candidate pool. Sure, you might get plenty of applicants who post for anything that's a promotion, but that's not what you want. You want people who are truly interested in the challenge presented and feel they can deliver on it. If you haven't spent the time to articulate that for them in a way that they can connect with and that gets them interested or even excited enough to apply, then what do you expect?

After working to ensure you've got the right requisition, you sort through all the resumes and have some promising candidates to interview. You now have thirty minutes or maybe an hour to establish a rapport, understand their experience, judge their truthfulness, and determine if they're a good fit for your team and the role. This is a significant hurdle for anyone to achieve in a short period of time and you're making one of the most important decisions you ever make in one segment of time spent together. How can you possibly do it? Those of us who have been hiring for some time have found what works, and while the approach you use will be customized to your personality the key questions you need to get answered are the same. You are looking to build a team that won't retreat. This means you need to understand three key elements about the person regardless of the seniority, job description, or if it's an individual contributor or people leader role:

- Resiliency and Growth
- Motivation
- Leadership Values

Resiliency and Growth

Question: *While we all like to talk about our successes, I firmly believe we learn the most when we fail. Tell me about a time you failed. What was the situation, what happened, and most importantly, what did you learn?*

Understanding how a candidate reacts when things go wrong is one of the most telling discussions in any interview. First, many people struggle to answer this question as they are afraid to admit the limits of their capabilities or where they have struggled in the past, as if admitting that they aren't perfect will somehow disqualify them from the role. Second, failure is guaranteed to happen at some point in your relationship, and learning how they reacted when it happened before can be an important insight.

The answers to this seemingly simple question will help you quickly develop a perspective on a potential team member. If they are unable or unwilling to give you an example, it's an indication that they are not willing to own up to their errors. This can be a warning sign as you seek to build a candid, open relationship with your team. It could also be an indication that they don't recognize when they make a mistake, which is even more worrisome. What is most important is not the situation that they share with you, but how they reacted to the failure. Hearing how they reflected on the event and what they took away from it will tell you much more about their future potential. If we can't identify and learn from our failures, how can we ever hope to grow and prevent it from happening again?

Finally, hearing about how people bounce back from hard times gives you a sense for their resiliency and adaptability. If they let a failure demotivate or prevent them from accomplishing the original challenge this is something that you would want to probe on further. You are looking to build a team that is willing to take on any challenge, risk failure, learn from that failure when it inevitability happens, and pick themselves up and try again. This is the foundation of a team that won't retreat and why this question is critical to identifying candidates with potential.

Motivation

Question: *What is it that gets you fired up, excited, and ready to get in the mix every day?*

How often do we interview someone, trying to understand everything about their experience and ability to tackle the challenges required, but never touch on if they would be motivated to actually do so? While we may talk about cultural fit, motivation is different. If someone is motivated by interpersonal relationships and team dynamics, yet the job requires a significant amount of time working alone, will they really be excited? This can also equally apply to the job responsibilities itself. If the role is support in nature, yet a candidate is motivated by making decisions about strategy, then this may be the wrong fit. Can you hope to retain them in this role or expect to see them over-perform if they don't even want to come to work to begin with?

While this question may seem very simple or even a "throwaway" question at first, it actually can quickly help you identify if you have a potential team member or not. The answer to this question, combined with your knowledge of the role specifics and work environment, will allow you to either clarify the reality to determine continued interest or know if you should consider a candidate whose motivating factors more closely mirror the role's nature. An intrinsically motivated team is critical to minimizing potential headwinds to success. Without an environment that motivates the team to tackle the challenges ahead, progress can quickly slow or even stagnate as time goes on or pressure builds. This is why you must consider what motivates a person when making a decision to offer them a place on your team.

Leadership Values

Question: *If you had to put your approach to leadership into a few bullets, what would they be? What elements or behaviors do you value most? Why?*

This question is one that tends to stump even the most articulate interviewee. It challenges them to concisely summarize what they value most both in a leader for themselves and also what they consider when leading others. While the application to people-leaders is clear, this is a powerful question for those who would be individual contributors as well. While many roles may not require formally leading a team, there are elements of leadership required for success no matter the position. Will the candidate be part of a product or project team? Do they need to influence others to achieve their objective? Even if the answer is no today, are you hiring for a job, or are you hiring for the future of your team? If you are treating your hiring decisions appropriately, then you're hiring for now and the future. With this in mind, do the person's leadership values match your own? Do they have the foundation of a compassionate leader waiting to be groomed and coached to their full potential?

While answers will vary, you should feel a connection with your own values as you listen to the candidate's answer. You will know within the first few sentences if this person carries the same principles of compassionate leadership or if their approach to leadership differs materially from your own. Regardless of their technical aptitude, you should seriously consider how this question is answered in making a hire decision as it also reflects on if this team member will value your leadership, mesh with a team built on a foundation of compassion, and respond to your coaching accordingly.

Similar to motivation, matching leaders to potential followers requires that their needs are satisfied. To understand how they want to be led requires us to ask and to know if we can successfully meet their needs. While we should never sacrifice the core tenants of compassionate leadership, part of serving your team is also to tailor your approach to the individual. This question will help you know if that's possible or if this may not be the best fit for them or you. Keep in mind your team is a reflection of you no matter their role. If they don't embody the same leadership values, your brand will be at risk.

Building a Team That Won't Retreat

————

Building a team that won't retreat takes time and requires you to hire with an eye to the future. You cannot sacrifice any one of these three dimensions if you want to build a team that is ready to take the field and stay there until the battle is won. They have to share your values as a leader (and be willing to follow as a result), be intrinsically motivated by their role, and handle failure in a productive manner with a growth-oriented mindset. If any one of these elements is missing, your team will begin to flounder when times of stress emerge. Failure will destroy their confidence. Productivity will decline to the minimally acceptable level over time, and your efforts to lead will be under constant attack. When times are good, these cracks in your team will be easily hidden and lull you into believing you have a team ready to tackle any challenge. It's in times of crisis that real leadership is required, and your investments in hiring a team that won't retreat will prove well made.

To repeat, the hardest decisions we make as leaders are who we hire and empower to do the job. When done right, it's also one of the most time-consuming activities we undertake. It can be easy to make compromises to reach the end, to close out the process, and to get a new person onboarded. This can be further magnified by your team's continued concern over the increased workload or concerns of hiring freezes on the horizon. While compromise is a part of the selection process, you must never be afraid to walk away and start over. The consequences of a bad decision are far-reaching and will take far longer to overcome than the delay experienced in restarting the process. Put differently, an empty chair is better than a wasted one.

6

THE CRITICAL RESOURCE

When asked what the most important resource or capacity constraint a leader faces today, many people focus on budget, headcount, knowledge resources, or any number of additional factors of production. However, the most critical and inflexible resource constraint any leader faces is time. They have a fixed number of hours in a day and week and must choose how to use them to the greatest advantage. Additionally, once an hour is spent it cannot be reclaimed. Accordingly, the most important resource that a leader must manage and jealously guard is his or her time.

You have significant demands on your time, whether it's staff meetings, strategy sessions, stand ups, control and compliance discussions, audit prep, media and governmental relations, customer experience deep dives, business review, continuity of business planning, talent reviews, or a myriad of other responsibilities. There is no shortage of people demanding your time and attempting to fill every slot on your calendar in a given week. You may view it as a sign of your importance when you don't have a free minute in any given day. This viewpoint would be misplaced, though.

As outlined earlier, a compassionate leader's primary job is to serve their team. How can you do this if you are spending your entire week in meetings that don't support this goal? This is not to say that you simply decline every meeting. No, there are many you do need to attend to both represent your team and gain valuable insights to prepare and protect them from potential problems. It is about how you rationalize which meetings you choose to attend, which ones you decline, and how you use the remaining time that is now available.

The Critical Resource

Take a look at your schedule for the next week. How much of your time is geared toward truly supporting your team? Is it ten percent? Twenty-five percent? If you spend twenty-five percent of your time on your team, this would mean you're spending ten hours a week. That may seem like a lot on the surface, but if you think about your primary job, which is to lead your team, shouldn't it be even more? This would mean you are spending two hours a day in one-on-one meetings with your directs, team reviews, skip level meetings, coaching and mentoring sessions, listening posts, or simply focused on the future. Yes, part of your job is to try and see what is coming so you can prepare your team for it. You have to spend time reflecting, reading, and trying to understand the implications of what is happening in both the macro and micro environments surrounding you. As discussed in Chapter 4, you must have a well founded belief about what the future holds.

Investing in Yourself

This requires a commitment to blocking time to focus. This is the hardest time to protect and ensure remains available for its purpose. Since you're not actually meeting with anyone, it's the first time that you might sacrifice when someone asks for an open slot. You cannot allow that to happen. You must treat your time focused on the future as a non-negotiable meeting with yourself. It's as important as any other meeting on your calendar, if not more. Time to think is critical to your ability to develop a strategy, to provide continued relevance to the firm, and thus to help prepare your team for the future.

Time spent on the future doesn't mean that's its unfocused. This is your time to invest in yourself as well as to plan. Leadership is an art form that is never truly mastered, but evolving every day. What people need is unique to their lives, and the approach one takes has to change to meet their needs. This means the compassionate leader can never stop investing in themselves, but must seek ways to further equip themselves to serve. This can take many forms, but at its core, it is about continuing to learn. Whether that's through reading books like this, studying trade journals, listening to podcasts, or reading periodicals that are relevant to your industry, what matters is that you continue to learn and think about how to both apply and share to the benefit of your team.

The Critical Resource

Be sure to cast a broad net when looking for areas of interest. Challenges to our teams and ourselves can come from any industry or geography in today's world. Political or social change, ecological concerns, technological disruption, changing demographic mix, recessionary risk, and changing customer preferences, to name a few, are all potential topics for consideration and study. Starting to spend time staying abreast of what's happening around the globe, and more tactically in your industry, will give you advantages many other leaders fail to grasp. This may sound daunting, but it's not intended to be an all or nothing list of topics. This is just a set of potential options for those of you who may not be investing your time today as you think about where to start.

Truly committing to this aspect of compassionate leadership may require you to dedicate part of your time away from the office to furthering your own knowledge. This is part of the sacrifice you make in the service of your team given the demands on each of us during the week. While initially it may feel like it's too much of commitment, soon it will just be part of your normal routine. For example, when you have coffee Saturday morning, instead of turning on the TV, pick up a magazine or newspaper whose views you value. Preferably, this should be one that gives a broad perspective on the world or industry and will challenge any pre-conceived beliefs you may have about a given topic.

Investing in Your Team

While the time spent investing in yourself is critical, perhaps the most valuable use of your time during each week is the time spent with your team in one-on-one or mentoring sessions. This time is centered on developing your team members for the future. It must be focused to ensure you maximize the value of the interactions, but don't be afraid to take some time to connect personally and check in. Challenge the mentee or team member to prepare the topics for discussion and come prepared to maximize their opportunity for feedback. These sessions should be about meeting their needs, not yours. If you have set the stage that your time is valuable, they won't waste it. If they do, then do not hesitate to remind them of your expectations and the trade off you are making by setting this time aside for them. Each minute spent with an individual who wastes it is a minute lost that could be used to help another. This investment of your time will yield dividends many times over as they continue to grow, can take on more responsibility from you, and allow you to further invest the added free time as you delegate additional activities.

While it may be tempting to focus solely on the near term opportunities for growth, mentoring sessions are a great opportunity to begin to understand your team's aspirations for the future. This may be within their current area of focus, in a new functional area, or in a completely different industry. Taking the time to help them identify and focus their goal creates a powerful connection between you and your team. Many of our team members don't truly know what they want to achieve initially beyond, "I want to get promoted." Part of mentoring is to challenge this broad, and frankly useless, goal to make it actionable and achievable.

For example, take an undefined goal of "promotion" and focusing the discussion on what job they really want. Do they want to run the firm, a business line, a functional area, or a team like yours? Is their dream to actually leave the firm to start their own business? While simple on the surface, this clarity will help you identify how to coach them effectively. Spending time helping your

61

mentee understand your industry more deeply won't be a good use of either person's time if they don't aspire to remain in the field.

Another powerful way to tackle the question of advancement is to focus your discussion on the individual's personal brand. Start by asking them what three to five characteristics they want to be known for within the firm. While a few iterations may be necessary to solidify the brand they want to establish for themselves, this will become a north star for how they operate each day. The problem with brand is that while we can articulate our desired reputation, it's others who decide what it actually is. This is why the next step in the process is to speak with others to understand how they are perceived today. Perception is reality, and understanding the changes required to establish the personal brand we want is a great starting point for a mentoring relationship.

Once you understand their goal, it is incumbent on you to marshal your abilities, connections, and knowledge to help them make progress against it. This may mean helping your team members find a new opportunity outside your organization. We shouldn't fear this potential outcome but embrace what it means. Losing people for the right reasons, in pursuit of their own happiness and career goals, is something to celebrate even if it hurts our personal performance in the short term.

Investing in Inclusiveness

As mentioned earlier, our world has become more polarized, and the middle ground an increasingly lonely place. If we're going to build a team in the truest sense of the word, they have to be bound not just with common purpose but also with faith and trust in each other. Creating this level of connection requires a leader who is willing to facilitate and engage personally in discussions on difficult topics when required. We cannot predict what types of world events might accelerate the need for this type of leadership, but when they occur we must be willing to answer the call. It can be tempting to try to sidestep the need, but your silence on issues that touch them personally will speak volumes to your team.

Facilitating a real discussion on topics that we have historically avoided cannot be undertaken without having firmly embedded a compassionate mindset within your organization. Without a concern for, and desire to, empathize with your teammates, attempts to challenge personal positions are futile. Individuals will dismiss the discussion and continue to fall back on their base position, never trying to understand an alternative point of view. It is important to identify when your team is ready to engage in a discussion toward a more inclusive and understanding dynamic. Assuming that you've established the foundations for meaningful dialogue, or events have created the necessity, it is up to you to both set the ground rules and at the same time model the behavior you hope to see.

While this will not be the case in all discussions, or for all team members, the emotional implications of opening yourself up are important to consider too. Don't be afraid to let people express their emotions, even if it's uncomfortable, as this is a powerful motivator for change. Many times they may be embarrassed, but it's up to you to validate what they are feeling and let them know that it's okay to bring that part of them to their work and the discussion. These types of discussions require a level of vulnerability, a belief that all participants have a positive intent, and the willingness to explore and, if appropriate, publicly acknowledge your personal shortcomings. These are some of the most difficult discussions to have for just this reason. The level of trust required to engage on difficult issues cannot be understated. You must request and be willing to grant everyone taking part the grace to express themselves in ways that may be not be as polished or "politically correct" as we might normally see. When we are exploring divisive subjects or challenging deep-seated beliefs we are interacting on topics in ways we may never have before and are bound to say something we don't intend. This is part of the learning process. We must be willing to explore new thoughts, revisit the rationale for our beliefs, and validate our thinking with others in the process. While necessary for change to occur, it requires all of us to accept that growth is not easy and can be messy at times.

When we can see the world through another's eyes it makes it real to us. Being touched by their stories or by the new understanding we now have is nothing to be embarrassed about. Our teams and workplaces offer us a level of diversity of thought, experiences, and backgrounds we likely do not experience anywhere else in our lives. It's amazing how much we can learn just by being willing to have a discussion we haven't had before. Even if we bring a deeper level of understanding and respect to one individual, the time spent has been invested well. You never know the impact you can have until you try, and it can yield meaningful results far beyond the doors of your office.

7

MISTAKES AND FAILURES

You've put in the time and energy to coach your team and have them functioning as a well-oiled machine. They continue to deliver release after release and then the inevitable happens. You get the call informing you that there is an issue. It doesn't matter how tenured or high performing your team is, mistakes and errors will happen. While we can work to mitigate the risk, we cannot eliminate them completely, no matter how much effort we invest in controls. Unfortunately, a lot of our control frameworks come from experience, and yes, our past failures.

As a compassionate leader, you will be challenged with more potential issues than many other leaders for a number of reasons. First, you have committed yourself to developing your team and helping them grow. Growth requires us to undertake new challenges and operate in areas we are not proficient. As failure often serves as the best teacher, you are bound to have a higher number of issues occur under your watch. The challenge for you is to create the environment that allows for growth and the associated mistakes to occur without adding undue risk to the firm. Establishing the proper monitoring and mitigation framework is a key prerequisite to enabling your team's development.

While putting people into unfamiliar situations without step-by-step guidance can serve as a powerful teaching tool, it requires, a more active engagement model in the short term. Setting aside time for more frequent meetings to review progress, decisions, and the associated rationale will be a required investment to enable the team to grow. Of course, these opportunities cannot be an excuse for allowing the control environment you've built to suffer. The goal is to allow your team to make small errors that they learn from while avoiding material issues in the process. Achieving this goal will also require you to suppress the urge to quickly redirect when your team is going astray. You must strike the balance of pointing them to the potential issue without telling them exactly what it is and how to avoid it. Leading them to the solution would create a dependency on you for direction as opposed to the desired outcome of empowered and self-reliant teams.

If you have succeeded in creating a culture where failure is expected, and accepted, your team will be willing to bring more items to your attention, instead of trying to resolve them without anyone being the wiser and potentially making things worse in the long term. While you don't actually *have* more issues than other leaders, you will hear about more of them. This is not a negative outcome of leading with compassion, but one you should embrace, even though on paper it may appear to be a poor result. While you may have more reported issues in total, you will have fewer significant items, as they'll be resolved sooner, and you will have the ability to leverage these opportunities for continued growth.

Mistakes happen. The question is how will you react when they do? While there will be rare scenarios that rise to the level of gross incompetence or intentional malfeasance, the vast majority of errors are unintentional, and the offending party feels terrible that it happened. They have come to you hat in hand apologizing for the error and wondering what to do next. These times are a moment of truth for you and your team. Do you lose your cool, yelling as you ask how they could have been so stupid as to let this happen? Perhaps you use some choice four letter words? This is the moment when your team will see if you are going to live what you preach.

No matter the severity of the issue, this is a time to keep your cool, objectively review the issue at hand, and determine what to do next. Losing your temper doesn't serve you or your team and in fact will have a lasting negative impact on your team's culture and future transparency. Handling the situation well, on the other hand, will result in continued transparency, which may prove critical to avoiding a career-ending escalation for yourself in the future. This doesn't mean you may not be disappointed with your team. But remember, you are responsible for everything that happens. You trusted them to complete the job successfully, so if they failed to do so, it was also your failure. This also applies to when you are reporting the issue to your leadership. Just as you claim the successes of your team to your benefit, you must also stand up and accept the blame for the failures as well.

The first thing to do when an issue arises is to focus on mitigation, but don't miss the opportunity to maximize the learning opportunity for your team. Their initial approach is likely to make you aware of the issue and ask what to do. Your reply should be to quickly refocus the discussion on what they think they should do next. While it may serve your sense of purpose or ego to have them dependent on you, creating a self-sufficient team is a hallmark of the compassionate leader. Have them outline the approach, explain their reasoning, and detail the risks that may arise. Validate or redirect as appropriate, but never forget to explain why you may think a different approach or consideration may be warranted. Remember, the goal whenever an error happens is to help the team learn from each failure.

Burn the Ships

Mistakes happen and our goal is not to punish our team, but to leverage each failure as a learning opportunity. How many times have we not taken full advantage of these opportunities, though? We're often on to the next deliverable, and focusing on what's behind us just isn't the most important item on our schedule for the day. However, focusing on what really happened is a critical step to our ability to maximize the value of mistakes we make. What was the real root cause? For example, was it as simple as a systems architect missing something in design?

Usually it's not, but we often stop here. There are times even our best and brightest make mistakes, but dig deeper: why did the architect miss it? Was it in how you articulated the ask? Did you even have the right ask to enable the team to catch this? Did you not ask the right question to allow the team to drill down? Where was your own knowledge about the business insufficient to be a good partner in the process? Think back over your own experiences. There have surely been items that have caused you problems repeatedly. Sharing these insights with your team will help prevent them from relearning the same lessons the hard way. What matters most when mistakes or failures happen is not what happened, but what we learned in the process. It's only when we honestly assess and learn from our past that we can change our future.

8

FATIGUE, EXHAUSTION, AND BURNOUT

While many of us want to pretend we are inexhaustible, always ready no matter what comes next, we have to accept that we are only human. No amount of caffeine can keep us running at full throttle every day, year after year. When you add to that times of crisis when even more is required, our teams and ourselves are bound to reach a point of potential collapse. There is a reason we get the best gas mileage at slower speeds than our vehicles are capable of. The harder the engine has to work, the more energy it has to consume, and consequently the quicker we run out of fuel. We are no different: our "tank" is just much bigger. We can operate successfully for long periods of time short of our maximum output. When pushed to the upper limit of our capabilities, the mental and physical energy required to maintain that pace rapidly depletes our reserves.

"Burn the Ships" leaders tend to ignore this concern until it's too late to reverse course. Recall that these leaders press on till the objective is secured and the victory won. The team is a tool to achieve their goal and casualties along the way are an acceptable outcome. We've discussed why this view must be discarded and the notion of our teams as easily replaceable resources abandoned. Part of your job as a compassionate leader is to monitor your team's "health." Not as a medical professional would, but in terms of their ability to continue to bounce back or take on new challenges. You know your team's strengths and weaknesses, and you also know when they are struggling to keep up. Throughout our careers, we will be asked to step up to support special efforts beyond our day-to-day, and we will also be faced with times of crisis where there is no option except to give more. During these times we cannot ignore any element of our team's performance as we have now asked them to give us all they have, and that will take a toll.

While we can perform at our max for a period of time, if we are not able to throttle back in a reasonable period, there are bound to be implications. The outcomes vary by individual, but the manifestation of fatigue will likely take one of these forms, in order of severity and a progression toward burn out:

1. *Increase in Error Rates* — When overtaxed or overwhelmed by the demands required of us, we quickly begin our own method of triage. The consideration of alternative outcomes or contingency planning is a casualty of the process. The possible but unlikely situations which could impact success are not cared for or even thought of in the first place as requests are transacted to quickly get to the next deliverable. We also tend to see an increase in self-inflicted or what we might call "stupid mistakes" creeping into our

performance. These types of errors can be just as detrimental to our firms if not identified and addressed quickly.

2. *Strong Performers Begin to Lag* — These are the team members you likely are leaning on most at any time, and even more so in times of crisis. Their commitment to growth and desire to be the "go to" person will start to lag as their own reserves are tapped. They will start to ask why you're giving more assignments to them, and it won't be perceived as a chance to demonstrate their potential, but a failure by you to distribute the work appropriately.

3. *Moderate or Complete Disengagement* — Disengagement could come in the form of medical leave, attrition, or a tipping point where performance declines significantly to meet the minimum expectation. This could also appear as a reduced commitment to arriving on time for meetings, call outs and unplanned absences, or no desire to offer suggestions or take on small but impactful assignments for the team.

Identifying the signs of fatigue and burn out in your teams is only the first step. If you've reached the point where you are seeing these behaviors, it's important you rapidly assess the situation and take action. You must take a more active role in helping them through to the other side. While each situation will be different, here are a few actions to consider:

- Can you break down the work in a way that makes it appear manageable and more easily checked off to maintain momentum? Seeing progress toward a goal is a powerful motivating force, and the more boxes we can check off as we go, the more achievable it appears.

- Provide more tactical direction and boundaries to help them stay focused on the "must-do." While micro-managing can be detrimental to high performing teams, in times of stress, making sure no effort is wasted takes priority in protecting your team from burn out. This must be a time bound action though, as leaders must return autonomy to their teams once a sense of normalcy has been restored.

• Go back to your roots and get in the dirt. This is an opportunity to show them why you are qualified to lead, and take on some of the work yourself. How can your functional expertise be brought to bear to lighten the load on your team? If you don't have the expertise, then take the administrative burden off them to let them focus. What reporting, presentations, meetings, et cetera can you do yourself? "All hands on deck" means you too.

• Review their deliverables and capacity or lack thereof, and help them prioritize, delay, or eliminate work. What's important in normal times may not be as high a priority in times of crisis. For example, do you really need Report X every Tuesday at 10? Without your direction, the team will continue to try and do it all to avoid disappointing you. You have to continually clarify your expectations for your team, especially as fatigue starts to take hold.

• Share a vision for the future. This rises in importance the longer our teams have to operate at max capacity. People begin to believe we'll never return to "normal." This can become a negative self-reinforcing narrative, serving to further accelerate their path to burn out and disengagement. You must remind them that we will get through this together and get back to an appropriate ongoing ask of them.

While ensuring your team is taken care of is critical, you also cannot ignore your own state of mind. You are just as susceptible to burn out as any member of your organization. In fact, taking care of yourself has to be your top priority. You know how far you can push yourself, where the limit lies, and the warning signs. These are different for everyone, but you know when you are starting to see the impacts on your daily life. Do you start losing your temper more quickly? Do things start frustrating you more than normal? Are you normally in the office early, but find yourself unable to get out of bed on time? Are you seeking unhealthy ways to release your stress? Does insomnia prevent you from recharging each night?

It's important to note that leading with compassion does not come without a personal cost to your emotional energy. The greater and more personal investment you've made in each of your team members will begin to take a toll. Connecting with and supporting the whole person, not just the professional, means you will more deeply relate in times of success, disappointment, or even tragedy. In one day you could support the mourning of a family member, celebrate a child's success, or hear about a new health issue, not to even mention what is happening in your own life which impacts your point of view before the first good morning is ever said. This roller coaster of emotions has an impact on your team and on you that cannot be ignored. Your ability to lead demands that you be emotionally ready to support your team when they come to you. This only increases the importance of constantly evaluating your own mental state, identifying the early signs of burnout, and knowing when you reach a point of exhaustion that impedes your ability to lead. You cannot lead others when you yourself are struggling to get through the day.

Dealing with your own fatigue can be challenging especially if you are attempting to change the culture of the broader organization to embrace compassion. Your boss may still subscribe to "Burn the Ships" principles and be focused only on the short-term outcome. The extreme divergence between Compassionate and "Burn the

Ships" Leaders will create an added personal stressor as you strive to protect your team and culture. The stress and temptation to stop buffering your team, to give in to demands regardless of the impact, will only increase as you begin to tire yourself, severely testing your commitment to compassionate leadership in the process.

These are just some examples, but the lesson is that you must honestly assess your own "health" on a regular basis. You may be tempted to never allow your team to see you hurting or exhausted; however, this would be a mistake. As discussed earlier, allowing your team to see your mistakes, failures, and even exhaustion strengthens your relationships over time. Just as you want to be there for your team, they want to be there for you. Don't be afraid to give them the chance to support you just as you would them. Allowing your team to step up and relieve some of your load will start to let you recover. At the same time, it will serve as a growth opportunity for members of your team to expand their knowledge and capabilities. While your team will allow you the freedom to step back, you still need to focus on yourself. Take real time off disconnected from the office, relaxing on a beach, hiking through the mountains, reading, exercising, working on a hobby, or whatever you've found that works best to free your mind and allow you to recharge. You must ensure you take full advantage of your leave. Time off is not a luxury, but a necessity if you are to lead your team to your maximum potential.

The closer you or your team get to burn out, the harder it is to recover. Like a medical condition, the sooner it is caught the easier it is to treat. Burn out is no different. The longer we wait to take action, the more dire the outcome. What could be worse than sacrificing our team, simply because we didn't take action early enough?

9

DEALING WITH THE INEVITABLE: WHEN PEOPLE LEAVE

If you have hired intentionally and are successfully leading, you will have created a highly respected and sought-after organization. You have been coaching and mentoring your team to grow beyond their current role and to embrace the principles of compassionate leadership in their lives. While a testament to your investment of time and energy in service to your team, this also means your people will be actively recruited by others throughout the firm. While your first instinct may be to protect your investment and prevent your team from leaving, you must fight this urge. Your efforts have not been in service to yourself, but to help them achieve their dreams. In many cases, this means taking on a role of greater responsibility or in an area that more closely matches their passions or interests. This is actually another measure of your success as a leader: to be known as a net exporter of talent.

To lose people for the right reasons is a powerful reinforcement and validation of your approach and leadership. You are spreading your beliefs, values, and culture far beyond what you could directly influence. The network effort of the people you have led going on to lead others will be a powerful multiplier and result in far more people benefiting from the principles you espouse. This means you will have to rebuild your team, but over time the pipeline of talent you have built will create natural succession plans for your own organization so that movement out creates opportunities within as well.

While these are positive scenarios and the ones we hope to see as leaders, there will be other times when we are faced with the more difficult decision of when to coach up or out. As a compassionate leader, our bias must be to coach up before considering a more radical solution, excepting material breaches in conduct which we cannot accept in any scenario. First, consider if the individual clearly understands the expectations and demands of them. It is your responsibility to effectively convey the expected standard of performance, and your initial response should be to reiterate and clarify accordingly. While the individual is ultimately responsible for their performance, the leader may also be at fault.

Yes, you must consider the initial point of failure to be your own. Have you provided meaningful and actionable feedback on the issues to no avail? Did you consider and explore if there is something happening in their life that's impacting their commitment or focus? Have you hired or placed someone into a role inappropriately, creating a job or culture mismatch? Did you fail to provide them the opportunities to continue to grow and develop, impacting motivation? These are just a few of the questions you must ask yourself to determine where the root cause of the performance issues may lie. It's always easy to blame someone else, but before moving forward with more permanent action, a compassionate leader must first challenge themselves and help the individual return to the expected standard.

Even if the fault lies with you for hiring incorrectly, there are times when there is no option but to consider parting ways with an individual. Accepting underperformance on your team is a cancer to your culture and your team at large. It cannot be tolerated for long or others will begin to resent carrying the extra load and blame you for allowing it to happen. You are not doing anyone any favors by keeping them around if they cannot perform to an acceptable standard, and it's up to you to make the hard decisions and take action accordingly. This is also compassionate leadership, even if it may not seem like it on the surface. The individual is not happy in their work, nor do they feel good about their contributions each day. The rest of your team is likely overtaxed, frustrated, and feeling like their interests are being sacrificed. If you are going to respect and protect your team, you must take action to enforce your shared standard and at the same time allow the individual to find work that will provide personal satisfaction, even if it means short term hardship.

Perhaps the most difficult exit for any leader is when economic situations require a reduction in team size due to no fault of any individual. Your primary job is to protect your team, and this feels like a betrayal of all you value, and a personal failure at the same time. Impacting the lowest performer on a high-performance team does nothing to rationalize what you have to do. At the same time, you rightfully worry about the larger team and the impact to your culture and their faith in your leadership, as you have failed in your part of the leader-follower pact. Handling these situations will take a significant toll on you personally while at the same time requiring you to leverage all of your skills as a leader.

First, you must be honest and open about the risks you see to the team as soon as you can. People need to prepare for the potential implications to their families and lives and you should give them as much notice as possible, even if it impacts the full team's performance in the short term. This doesn't mean they will personally be affected, but acting with transparency and showing you care for them as people before employees will further reinforce your right to lead. Next, you must come to terms with why this is happening yourself. How does this reduction, while extremely difficult for all involved, serve the broader team? Does it allow the rest of your team to retain their roles and ability to provide for their families? You must honestly believe this yourself, and if you don't, have the courage to discuss the rationale with your leadership. Conveying messages you don't believe in will be evident and undermine your credibility with the team. This can have long lasting implications for your culture and your team's commitment in the future.

When you actually have to communicate with the impacted individuals, make sure to honor their contributions, be direct, and treat them respectfully. Understand that this is not just a professional parting, but one that is highly personal too. Do everything you can to allow them time to say goodbye to their colleagues and friends. You have trusted these people with the firm's assets, its reputation, and personally you have trusted this person with your brand and authority. Just because you now have to part ways doesn't change any of that. Once all communications have been completed, take the time to tell the broader team it's over. You must establish that this time is behind us and we're moving forward together. Restoring a feeling of security for your team must be your first priority.

While most leaders will have to face this situation at some point in their career, you should also do everything you can to avoid it in the first place. As discussed, part of your role as the leader is to have a view for the future. This does not just apply to trends outside of the firm, but inside as well. Your team is depending on you to keep your head up, see the clouds gathering, and start preparing for the coming storm. When you start to see this happening, either at a macro or micro level, you have to be even more intentional about your organizational design and hiring. As opportunities arise, should you backfill the role? Can you consolidate roles to offer growth opportunities? Is it better to absorb the work, increasing the load on the remaining team, to prevent an action later on as you have an open position to offer instead of a person? Given the turnover in most organizations, this is an easily leveraged tactic, but requires you to be forward looking and willing to accept some frustration for the longer term benefit. While you may be wrong, it's absolutely worth delaying a hire rather than terminating someone later because you hired just before a force reduction. It is the height of compassionate leadership to protect those who work for you in times when jobs are eliminated. If you are successful in protecting your team, they will never know it, but leadership is not about recognition. It's about service to those who choose to follow.

10

HOW THE COMPASSIONATE LEADER BENEFITS

Most of this book has been focused on the significant effort and sacrifice required of you to lead with compassion in today's world. Some of you may be asking yourself why you'd put yourself through the challenge of applying these principles successfully when the "Burn the Ships" approach has worked just fine for you till now. You also know something has been missing from your own life, though, most likely in how you have been led yourself. It's often easy to identify what we don't like, but not so easy to know how to change it. That's what compassionate leadership is. It's a counter force in a world that abandons us all. It's the thing that you couldn't place your finger on, but once you start to apply its principles you'll quickly start to realize this is the change you want to see in our offices. Choosing to embrace this philosophy is also choosing to actually lead. To reject what we see as normal or acceptable and be willing to challenge the status quo. To take a stand that you will make your team's lives better than anyone else who could sit in your seat.

Challenge and Meaning

The chance to be a change leader, especially a cultural one, is an exciting challenge to undertake. It can be its own motivating force and reward in knowing that what you are doing every day will make a difference in people's lives. This is what we all desire at our core: for our lives to have meaning, so that others will remember us when we're gone. Being willing to care for the whole person, to build a deeper connection, to support their dreams, and to protect them from the wolves within our firms creates a personal legacy. A relationship that transcends the day to day interactions you have with your team. One that will inspire them to be their best self. You will be admired and remembered as a meaningful influence in their lives.

Execution and Delivery

Leaders who hire and coach teams that won't retreat will naturally achieve greater executional success. Target dates will be met with greater frequency while their organizations will absorb the challenges of difficult times without impacting their commitments. The greater level of collaboration and support for one another will manifest itself in numerous ways that benefit the organization at large. Teams will also see fewer political games, less jockeying for position, and fewer instances where people try to hoard information to enhance their contribution. When issues do invariably occur, they will be quickly escalated for review and remediation. Team members will not waste time trying to fix it themselves to avoid blame and potentially make the issue significantly worse. Issues thrive with time, but a culture of compassion will ensure they have very little time to grow unchecked. A transparent, open team and a reputation for delivery are two very tangible benefits compassionate leaders accrue.

Connection and Inspiration

It could be in pursuit of a shared vision, or as a result of a personal relationship, but compassionate leaders create connections with their teams that transcend contractual relationships. These connections could be based on any number of different foundations, but at its core there is an element of inspiration. Inspiration drives people to give more of themselves. This results in a higher level of commitment, critical thinking, and passion than any other motivating or coercive force, directly translating to your own success.

Personal Brand

Leading with compassion is also a way for you to stand out in a crowd. You are operating in a way that people aren't used to seeing, and this will cause them to talk. Your reputation will quickly grow throughout the firm and everyone will want to work for you. They will seek out the opportunity to move into your organization and as a result you will have your choice of talent. This is the best position to be in as you will have no shortage of qualified candidates waiting in the wings. Your success is determined by your team, so be the leader that draws talent to you, not one that is forced to go out and find it.

Talent and Followership

If you apply these principles consistently you will build a following in a significant and sustainable way. As you move to take on new opportunities, you will have your choice of people who will want to work for you again. This will allow you to build a strong team immediately or seed new organizations with talent that you can depend on to help you build your culture. Similarly, this will allow you to be a culture carrier for the organization who trains and exports talent, influencing the firm far beyond your scope of responsibility as outlined on the org chart. Everyone knows who the real leaders of a firm are, and many times they aren't the people with the titles.

Your investments in your team will also build a following in a significant and sustainable way. Voluntary attrition will decrease and you will only lose your team members to the right opportunities.

How the Compassionate Leader Benefits

While the benefits of eliminating attrition are immense, stability within your organization will also allow you the opportunity to continue to grow yourself. Less time spent tactically means more time mentoring, investing in yourself, and establishing a strategic vision. This is how you prepare yourself for the next promotion and opportunity to lead at a more significant level.

When Opportunities Arise

The final, and most personally impactful, benefit is when others recognize the impact of your leadership and want it for their own organization. Over time you will find yourself in demand and have a number of opportunities presented to you. While flattering, the challenge lies in determining what role to accept. How should you decide if the job is worth accepting when setting aside compensation as the determinate factor? When evaluating a potential change, there is a three prong test that can prove valuable in trying to determine if it's the right move:

Question: *Do I add more value to the organization in this role than in my current one?*

While we may not think about it explicitly, it's important to leave the office feeling like we've made a difference and earned our salary. A sense of purpose is critical to maintaining motivation, so you should honestly evaluate if you'll add more value in the proposed role than you currently do. While it may sound appealing to earn more, or even the same, salary for less work, you will quickly find yourself unfulfilled and seeking a change. This is clearly not in the best interest of you, your team, or your employer.

Question: *Will I continue to learn and grow in this role?*

This question focuses on our inherent motivation and innate desire to avoid stagnation. When we stop learning, it's a good indication it's time to move on. When evaluating a new role it's important that we bring a strong foundation, but we should also need to to grow ourselves to master it. Whether it's a new industry, product, or functional area, look for a role that requires you to develop yourself. This will serve to further increase your skillset and prepare you for a greater variety of roles, while at the same time motivating you to invest the time to become an expert in your new field. Taking on a role which doesn't require personal growth is the beginning of the end for your career.

Question: *Do I respect who I will work for and believe they will give me credit for the value I add?*

Asking yourself this question helps you determine if this role reports to someone who shares your commitment to compassionate leadership. If you have embraced these principles, you will never want to serve another who does not. As mentioned earlier, followership is a choice. This is your time to determine if you want to follow. Failure to consider this question and choosing to work for a "Burn the Ships" leader is a disaster waiting to happen. While it may work at first, over time the frustration, stress, and value mismatch will drive a wedge in your relationship. The only option when this happens is to seek another job change, potentially impacting your career trajectory.

———

Burn the Ships

While not always within your control, especially when considering a move to a new firm, honestly evaluating these questions will quickly help eliminate roles that may seem attractive but will fail to provide personal satisfaction over the long term. While one of the most personally satisfying benefits of compassionate leadership is being sought out for new roles, don't allow the validation of your approach to lead you to accept the wrong role. Leaving your team is not a decision to be taken lightly and making sure you do it for the right reasons is critical to your future success.

CLOSING THOUGHTS

Throughout this book I've tried to make a case for why we need more compassionate leaders in our organizations. I am not the first to advocate for this type of change, but each voice we add enhances the call to action, bringing us one step closer to the tipping point where the status quo itself has changed. The "Burn the Ships" approach to leadership is failing our teams, our families, and our firms. It is only a matter of time before this short-term, consequences be damned mindset not only causes us to lose our talent, but also begins to materially impact the sustainability of our enterprises in the process.

While I have focused on how compassionate leadership requires us to give more of ourselves to our teams, I don't mean to imply that it means you have to be selfless or have no ego. We all are motivated by different factors, and motivation to be recognized or rewarded is not at odds with a compassion mindset. It's how we manage that part of us that matters. We begin to see that this is not a zero-sum game where for one to succeed another must fail, and in the process recognize that our ability to give to others far exceeds our capacity to take from them.

When your career is over and you think back on all you've accomplished you likely won't remember hitting that revenue target that no one thought was possible. While it may seem like the most important thing in our lives at the time, *what* we achieved is quickly forgotten. We remember *who* we met along the way: the people we spent time truly getting to know throughout our career; colleagues we stood side by side with as we fought to achieve what might have seemed impossible; mentors who invested in us and our potential when there was nothing in it for them. This is compassionate leadership in action: a focus on the people we are here to serve and who come to work each day striving to meet the standard we set.

It seems daunting at first, but the example you set, the investments you make, and the care you inject into your teams will have a greater impact than anything else you do. Over time, it will become second nature and you'll start to forget there was ever another way. Your efforts will have a network effect as those you lead go on to head their own teams, taking the principles you taught with them, furthering your legacy of leadership, and benefiting people you will never meet. This is a legacy we can rightfully take pride in, and when our work is done we can rest easy knowing that we truly did make a difference in people's lives.

**Leadership is not a privilege, but a duty.
Leaders are not empowered, but entrusted.
Leadership is service to those who choose to
follow.**

A NOTE FROM THE AUTHOR

Though I didn't realize it at the time, this book has been in the works my entire life. Learning how to lead is not a journey we begin once we start working full time, but something we begin to understand much earlier in our lives. We see leadership modeled by others at every stage of our development and we quickly learn both what works, but more importantly what feels right. Discovering the type of leader you want to be is a process that takes years and one that is never completely finished. It is influenced by leaders you respect and also those you do not want to follow. Your beliefs and approach will be refined by the authors you read, conversations you have, and what you experience as you attempt to lead others. My journey has been no different. I would not have been able to write this book without the contributions of many over the course of my life.

Like most things in life, the foundation for my approach to leadership comes from my parents. While they taught me many things, one of the most impactful has been the humility to accept that we never achieve anything without the support and sacrifice of others. As Dr. Edward Judson is quoted as saying, "If we succeed without suffering, it is because someone has suffered before us; if we suffer without success, it is because someone will succeed after us."[9]

While there are too many to name without inadvertently failing to acknowledge someone, I cannot thank enough all those who have invested in me over the years. Though there was nothing in it for them personally, their support, challenges, and

[9] *University of Chicago Sermons*. United States, University of Chicago Press, 1915.

insights have helped me become the leader I am today. At the same time, I am especially grateful for those I've had the privilege to lead and mentor. Colleagues and friends who have understood when I have failed to live up to the bar I've set, who have lifted me up when I've struggled, and who have allowed me to refine who I am as a leader alongside them. A special thanks to those who repeatedly asked, "So when are you going to write a book?"

Finally, my wife, Breana, without whom this book would likely have remained a dream. I've learned that attempting to write a book intended to help others can quickly test your confidence. Her unwavering encouragement and reassurance when I would question myself were instrumental in completing this endeavor. If that wasn't enough, she also undertook the especially challenging job of editing my writing.

A Note From the Author

I hope this book has helped you in some way on your journey. If it has, please pass it on to someone else, so that together we can help many more leaders adopt the principles of compassionate leadership to the benefit of our teams and organizations.

———

Andrew
leadingwithcompassion@gmail.com

ABOUT THE AUTHOR

Andrew S. Keen has spent eighteen years in Financial Services learning how to build and lead successful teams. Over his career, he has come to understand that traditional management practices are failing our organizations. He has seen firsthand the power of follower-focused, compassionate leadership as he directed thousands of people across seventeen countries.

Andrew earned a Bachelors degree in Management from Georgia Tech before going on to receive his M.B.A from the University of North Florida. While he does not consider himself an expert, he simply seeks to share what he has learned and hopes it will have a positive impact on how people are led across our firms.

Made in the USA
Monee, IL
30 April 2023

32646659R00069